Table of Contents

Introduction

When a child is diagnosed with autism, most parents have no idea what this means for them and their child. Like most parents of autistic children, they knew that something was different about their child's development, but couldn't put a finger on it. A diagnosis of autism can raise many questions for a parent:

What is autism?

How does autism affect my child's life?

What does it mean for me raising a child with autism?

How should I behave?

Does our life change?

Is my child disabled?

Is it my fault?

Am I a bad parent?

How should I behave?

Can autism be cured?

Can my child live a normal life?

Autism is not well understood in our society, and most parents don't know anything about autism before their child is diagnosed. Loneliness and fear of the unknown can wear you down, but information about autism helps alleviate some of it. For the parent of an autistic child, knowledge truly is power, as it helps them understand how to approach the child and handle their own mixed emotions.

Donna Williams, in her book. "Somebody Somewhere" describes autism thus:

> *"… Autism makes me feel sometimes that I have no self at all and I feel so overwhelmed by the presence of other people that I cannot find myself. Autism can also make me so totally aware of myself that it is like the whole world around me becomes irrelevant and disappears."*

Donna was diagnosed as autistic in her mid to late twenties. Until then she was assessed and labeled as psychotic, deaf, retarded and severe emotionally retarded. Even though she grew up in an abusive environment and left home at the age of 15, she managed to graduate with a Bachelor of Arts and obtained a Diploma of Education. In spite of being a child who only managed to talk in sentences at the age of 9, and who made up characters in order to adapt to different social circumstances, nowadays she is a well known artist, sculptor, composer, screenwriter, and an internationally best-selling author. With her four autobiographical books about autism, she helps us to understand the struggle that people with autism face in order to merge their world with the wider world.

Donna Williams, Temple Grandin, Liane Holliday Wiley, (12, 13, 23, 24, 25) have shared their stories and experiences of autism. Their works suggest that the best way to understand autism—and the needs of a person with autism—is by understanding their different way of thinking and perceiving the world, rather than labeling their behaviors as deviant.

How did these exceptional people manage to make it, and eventually help us to understand the puzzle of autism?

One major element is to understand how the different communication channels that children with autism use to make them feel safe in a strange world. Temple Grandin refers to this need in Oliver Sacks' book "An Anthropologist to Mars" (18) Temple Grandin, as a child, had a deep desire to have a close friend. She couldn't explain what made other children feel distant. Although she was admired for her brilliance, she couldn't connect with others. She mentions that it took her years to understand how difficult she found it, to be aware of all the different social signals. Even now, she tries her best to deal with social conditions that other people find simple. She realizes how hard it is to for people like her to survive in what seems, to them, a rather strange world.

Essentially, autism is a pervasive developmental disorder affecting many aspects of a child's functioning. Even in children who are of normal nonverbal intelligence, social and communicative development is disrupted. Aspects of the child's functional system that are typically affected are:

- Recognition and Comprehension

- Sense of self

- Sense of others

- Cognitive visualization

- Sequencing and categorization

- Synthesis and analysis

- Retrieval skills relating to information on sensory, emotional, social, cognitive level

Despite difficulties in fundamental areas as sensory processing, speech and language, and social interaction skills, autism is a complex and enigmatic disorder that can offer gifts as well. We need to remember that every child is different, and the challenge is to get to know their unique strengths and limitations. Children with autism can show special talents in a variety of areas, including rote memory abilities, calculation skills, and artistic and musical talents.

Even for children whose intelligence is normal or below normal, these interests—even when not exceptional—are a source of calmness and occupation. When you raise a child with autism, it is helpful for your relationship to keep that in mind. This book takes the autistic experience as an example, and it promotes understanding autism in all its fierce glory.

Every child, autistic or not, needs to be accepted and loved. Even if autism is part of your child, it is not all of his/her personality. She/he still has personal beliefs, emotions, interests, and preferences like any other person. Autism is not chosen by either the parent or the child; but a child with autism needs to be loved unconditionally, just like their non-autistic counterparts. Your child just needs more patience, and you need more support, when coping with autism.

This book intends to inform you about autism. It's a starting point for parents whose children have just been diagnosed as autistic, by helping them understand the world of an autistic mind. Even for parents who have already read books about autism, this book may give you further insight into autism. The book aims to help you make sense of what you already know from your experience of raising an autistic child. Of course, we cannot replace or substitute medical or therapeutic programs or the knowledge of your therapists, who know your child individually. But this book can give you a lot of ideas and strategies to help you cope well with your child. The most important agenda of this book is to afford you a better understanding of how your children think and perceive the world.

Defining autism is the first important subject that will be addressed. In the first chapter, we will cover the varying degrees of impairments of children who are diagnosed with autism. Although this book is not meant to be theoretical, reviewing some basic concepts will bolster your understanding of the condition.

There are a lot of myths surrounding autism that should be set aside. It is often observed that mixed feelings, guilt or misconceptions parents carry as a result of such myths weigh them down. Thus, the second chapter will focus on busting some of the more prominent myths.

Chapter Three is about the triad of impairments that comprise the clinical identity of autism. It covers the qualitative deviation in social interaction, social communication and symbolic play. These behavioral patterns should not be considered just in terms of deficits, and this chapter aims to help parents to understand that children with autism have a different way of thinking and learning—the "autistic" way of learning.

Although the basic cause of autism is still unknown, Chapter Four will review a number of studies that refer to suspected causes of autism. Instead of discussing these studies academically, we will explain these suspected causes in a way that helps parents become fully informed, and frees them of guilt or misconceptions of bad parenting.

Chapter Five describes the passage from diagnosis and assessment, to application of educational methods that promote the understanding of the autistic way of thinking. Emphasis is given to applying treatment methods that shed light on the autistic way of thinking.

Chapter Six is all about managing different strategies. This includes strategies that help in managing important issues that a parent deals with on a day-to-day basis, such as medical issues, seizures, regression, behavioral problems, medication, sleep disturbances, sibling and family issues, and sensory issues.

Chapter Seven will focus on the description of the grief cycle, a theory that encourages parents to accept their child's uniqueness and deal with their own mixed feelings.

Finally, Chapter Eight describes some guidelines for parenting a happy—if autistic— child in a healthy family system.

Chapter 1
What is autism?

The word "autism" comes from the Greek word "autos" meaning self. Before 1943, some scientists used the term autism to describe symptoms of schizophrenia or severe intellectual disability. Autism as we know it now was first described in 1943 by Leo Kanner, and then in 1944 by Hans Asperger. The two doctors were working independently of each other, but they happened to identify a common set of clinical characteristics among the children being studied. They both used the same term to describe enigmatic children who seemed to be absorbed in their own world. According to Kanner, the main characteristics of autism include severe social impairment, lack of communication, rigidity of thought, and ritualistic patterns of behavior. Asperger, on the other hand, studied children with exceptional abilities and usually an average or high intelligence, but with deficits in social communication. Even today, the scientific community commemorates Dr. Asperger by using the term "Asperger's syndrome" to describe children with normal or high intelligence and autistic characteristics. (1, 8, 26)

Can autism be defined?

George is 4 years old. He loves swimming, spinning, jumping on his trampoline, going for long walks, singing and tickles. He has an incredible memory and he instantly learns everything he is taught. He looks like an angel. He is non-verbal, but he can tell you everything with his sparkling eyes, says his mother. She always felt that something was different with this child. When George was first diagnosed, she thought it was the 'flu and she wondered how he would get over it. When she first heard that autism is a neurodevelopmental disorder, and that it cannot be cured, she felt devastated. Today she is a proud mum who sometimes feels tired, raising an autistic child, but mostly she feels blessed, as she has George with the sparkling eyes in her arms.

When you first hear the word "autism" you may want to ignore it. Most parents do. A diagnosis of autism is difficult to accept, and parents react differently depending on their personality and adaptivity. Some parents begin to research and look for the best way to help their children. Other parents pretend that nothing has happened and avoid dealing with their mixed emotions. Others feel desolate and try to hide it from their social circle. There are parents who try to dispute the diagnosis. As a consequence, they start visiting one specialist after another till they hear what they want—that their child doesn't have autism.

On first hearing this diagnosis, it's very important for a parent to become fully informed about autism. Autism is actually a range of complex neurodevelopmental disorders rather than being just one thing. Disorders within the autistic spectrum comprise Classic Autism, Asperger's syndrome, Heller syndrome and Rett syndrome. Being developmental disorders, they influence the way the child conceptualizes experiences and knows him/herself and the world. Behavioral patterns for these children cannot be explained in terms of deficits. Rather, they are mainly explained as a different way of thinking and learning.

These patterns characterize the clinical entity of autism which comprises the triad of impairments as introduced by Lorna Wing. This concept of the triad includes a qualitative deviation of social interaction, social communication, and restricted, repetitive stereotyped patterns of behavior and restricted interests and activities. The presentation of autistic behavior varies among individuals. Even in the same individual, the clinical picture differs from time to time, depending on age and mental capability. For the above reason, we speak of the "autism spectrum" which encapsulates the natural and inherent variation of the same handicap across people and across time. This means that although all people with autism share certain difficulties, their condition will affect them in different ways. Some people may live independently, but others may need lifetime support. Some people speak, others do not. Some people experience over sensitivity to external stimuli, but others don't.

These definitions of autism are useful in obtaining an in-depth understanding, but sometimes you may find yourself in the difficult position of having to explain in simple words what autism is. You may be asked by your child with autism, his/her siblings, by relatives, or by friends. Parents wonder how to explain autism in a non- academic way. Sometimes they try to describe the definition of autism as they read it or as they have heard it, but they fail to do it well. Instead of taking the academic route, speaking from the heart using simple words is often the most effective way to explain what autism is. In essence, autism is a disorder that makes it hard for people to deal with the world around them, and so they prefer to keep their distance form others. This is not because they don't want other people's company, but they don't know how they should interact with them. Sometimes, a touch or a hug is snubbed by them, not because they find it annoying but because it causes them feel pain. A doorbell could jar them as much as an annoying honk of a car. It's like wearing your shoes on the wrong feet. Such a child-friendly definition of autism makes it easier for everyone to empathize with the behavior of children with autism. (1, 8, 26)

Chapter summary

Autism is a range of complex neurodevelopmental disorders. Disorders within the autistic spectrum comprise—beyond classic autism—Asperger syndrome, Heller syndrome and Rett syndrome. Autism comprises the triad of impairments introduced by Lorna Wing. This concept of the triad includes a qualitative deviation of social interaction, social communication and restricted, repetitive, stereotyped patterns of behavior and restricted interests and activities. Autism influences the way the child conceptualizes experiences and knows the self and the world. Qualitative deviation and autistic symptoms are of organic etiology. Autistic characteristics cannot be explained in terms of deficits. They are mainly explained in a different way of thinking and learning—the autistic way of thinking. Even if all people with autism share certain difficulties, their condition will affect them in different ways.

Chapter 2
Myths surrounding autism

There are a lot of myths and misconceptions about autism that can misinform or mislead you. It's important to free yourself from unnecessary misconceptions that could affect your relationship with your child. we have listed the most common myths with their corresponding facts in this chapter. (1, 8)

Diagnosis

Myth: Autism is a disease.

Fact: Autism, just like dyslexia isn't a disease. It's a developmental disorder.

Myth: It is better to "wait and see" if a child does better.

Fact: Early diagnosis and intervention is found to contribute to better outcomes. The sooner a child is diagnosed, the better for the child's development.

Cause

Myth: Autism is contagious.

Fact: Neither you nor your partner give your child autism. In the same way your child can't catch autism from, or give it to, other children. Autism is a disorder that some people are born with.

Myth: Autism is caused by vaccines.

Fact: Although some studies seemed to indicate a relationship between vaccines and autism, this has been disproved. Vaccines protect your child from serious diseases. Autism is a neurodevelopmental condition that existed before most of the current vaccines were even introduced.

Myth: Autism is caused by poor parenting, or the parent's behavior.

Fact: Although the exact cause of autism is unknown, it has been consistently proven that parental behavior before, during, or after pregnancy does not cause autism.

Behavior

Myth: Autism is a tragedy.

Fact: Admittedly, autism is challenging to deal with. But by attending appropriate intervention programs and increasing your personal and emotional awareness, you can adjust to the new challenges of raising a child with autism. If you see your child as disabled, they will be disabled.

Myth: Autism means not being able to speak.

Fact: Difficulty in communication is one of the symptoms of autism. This doesn't mean that children with autism can't speak. Only 15-20% of people with autism don't develop speech. Even these people usually develop alternative ways of communication using symbolic systems, (MAKATON, PECS), augmented communication devices, or computers. With early identification and intervention, chances of effective speech can be improved significantly.

Myth: Autism is associated with intellectual disability.

Fact: About 15 – 25% of autistic people are intellectual disabled, but most don't. Some people with autism also demonstrate superior intelligence. The communication problems that autistic people usually have are unrelated to intellectual disability.

Myth: Children with autism lack empathy and affection.

Fact: Empathy is the ability to understand the emotional state of others. People with autism are not robots. They can recognize the emotional state of others, they just can't respond to complex social contexts, and often find it difficult to show an emotional response similar to other people. This doesn't mean that they are empty of emotions.

Myth: Children with autism cannot learn.

Fact: Children with autism have different learning styles. Some are kinesthetic learners, others are visual or auditory learners. Given the right kind of inputs, any children with autism can learn.

Myth: Children with autism don't make eye contact.

Fact: Although there is frequently a lack of eye contact in children with autism, many children with autism make eye contact as they become more comfortable with others.

Myth: Children with autism demonstrate disruptive behaviors.

Fact: Tantrums, hitting, or throwing items need to be explained by the light of events, and not as a result of autism. Such behavior needs to be seen as a call for attention, or as a difficulty in responding to social stimuli.

Myth: All children with autism have sensory issues.

Fact: Sensory impairments are not a part of the diagnostic criteria for autism, although a significant number of children with autism have sensory issues. However, not all children with autism demonstrate sensory issues or repetitive body movements.

Treatment

Myth: Autism is a torture and autistic children live a life suffering from autism.

Fact: Prejudice and discrimination make people with autism suffer, not the condition. They suffer when they feel isolated from social, educational or occupational environments, or when other people make decisions for them without involving them. Autism can be managed better if people with autism feel accepted.

Myth: Autism can be cured.

Fact: Autism is a life-long developmental disorder. You cannot grow out of autism or cure a child with medical or alternative therapies. But age appropriate educational programs help in managing many autistic symptoms. Through these, the child can learn how to adjust to different environments.

Myth: Certain intensive behavior programs can cure autism.

Fact: There is no treatment or educational program that can 'cure' autism. Early behavior-based educational programs have a positive effect on some children. The educational programs that would be chosen need to be individualized as they have different effects on children.

Myth: Autism is cured with special diets.

Fact: Special diets may help a child show progress, but no diet can replace an educational treatment program. None of these diets get rid of autism, they just help the child feel better.

Chapter summary

There are a lot of myths and misconceptions about autism, and it helps to look past these sometimes enticing but useless notions.

Parents should be informed about myths and facts about autism diagnosis, causes, behavior and treatment to help them make the best choices for their child.

Chapter 3
What are the symptoms of autism? The triad of impairments

Lorna Wing, an English psychiatrist and a pioneer in the field of child development, contributed to the understanding of the autism spectrum disorders by introducing the term "the triad of impairments". After conducting an epidemiological study, she found up that social impairment is a disorder of development and although there are different manifestations, they all are part of autism. There are three areas of development associated with social communication that are impaired, and which together consist of the triad of impairments. This triad of impairments that Wing and Gould introduced in 1979 is the backbone of autism diagnosis even today.

This triad of impairments refers to a qualitative deviation of social interaction, social communication, and social understanding and imagination (including symbolic play/restricted repetitive and stereotyped behavioral patterns/restricted interests and activities). As a parent, you are the first to notice these deviations in your child. Recognizing your child's difficulties associated with social behavior can help provide an early diagnosis and intervention. Keep in mind that these impairments affect the way your child perceives the world, and are not by themselves indicative of the child's intelligence. Understanding the way in which your children react because of social impairments promotes the learning process as you can be familiar with his/her learning style.

Social Interaction

As Kanner has described, a child with autism interacts with others in what can seem like, an odd way.

> "He paid no attention to the persons around him. When taken into a room, he completely disregarded the people and instantly went for objects, preferably those that could be spun. Commands or actions that could not possibly be disregarded were resented as unwelcome

intrusions. But he was never angry at the interfering person. He angrily shoved away the hand that was in his way or the foot that stepped on one of his blocks…"

Does your child seem aloof? Is he/she passive? Does he/she seem not to join in an activity, and remain at a distance? Do you feel that you try too much to encourage him/her to engage in a social activity? Even when he/she is active, does he/she engage in the activity in an odd or different way? Do you notice that when he/she does join in with full energy and enthusiasm, he/she tends to violate some unwritten rules of social interaction?

You may find yourself wondering why your child's behavior is characterized by an apparent lack of responsiveness to others, or a lack of awareness of cultural norms. Children with autism may treat other people as inanimate objects, and they may seem to not have empathy for others. Some of them have atypical eye contact, and they may avoid developing common interests with others. They often face difficulties in recognizing social signs and conventions. This lack of shared attention to social stimuli that characterizes children with autism tends to result in limited engagement in early social experiences. Social signs are like a puzzle that is just beyond their grasp for these children. This is why social interaction often seems too complicated and puzzling for your children. Consequently, their capacity to respond to pertinent information is diminished, and they can't communicate their intentions or share meanings effectively.

Children with autism interpret social life like a complicated game in which they are the only who haven't been told the rules. This game isn't like chess, with strategies and logical movements, but has complex—often contradictory —social content. Imagine how hard your life would be without knowing what to do when you feel angry, happy or embarrassed. Imagine how difficult it would be if you couldn't figure out what your friend thinks, believes, and feels, or if you couldn't explain the way you do! It's how we feel if we close our eyes and try to move in a dark room. Having autism is like being socially blind in a world full of social cues!

Social Communication

Do you see your child's difficulties with verbal and non verbal communication or the relationship between them? Does he/she find it hard to fully understand the meaning of common gestures, facial expression or tone of voice? Have you ever heard your child counting from one to five without understanding the reason or the context? Children with autism develop deviant language and communication abilities. It seems confusing for them to comprehend the semantic and pragmatic aspects of language. They may say things that seem out of context when trying to have conversations with others.

These children are literal and they often misinterpret the figurative form of speech. Their comments aren't always related to the situation and they talk incessantly without interpreting other people's responses. For nonverbal autistic children, challenging behaviors are a means of getting the attention they want and having their needs met.

For verbal children with autism, the language development can be uneven. They might rapidly develop a strong vocabulary in the area of their interest, or be able to read words before the age of five. On the other hand, they don't always comprehend what they have read. They don't instantly respond to others and there are times that they don't correctly interpret what they hear. Some children are able to hold an unstoppable monologue about an issue that he/she likes, but aren't able to share this interest by making it a two way conversation even on the same topic. Many parents visit doctors because they believe that their children have hearing problems.

This doesn't mean that they don't have the desire to be with others. Some children speak in a high-pitched voice or robot-like speech, or use stock phrases to start a conversation. This must be recognized as signs of them wanting to communicate. So a "Hi" for this child isn't just a greeting.

Myles and Simpson explain this complexity at their article 'Understanding hidden curriculum'.

> "A greeting... is a social skill that is thought to be simple. However, further analysis shows this skill, which most take for granted, to be extremely complex. How a child greets a friend in the classroom differs from type of greeting that would be used if the two met at the local mall. The greeting used the first time the child sees a friend differs from the greeting exchanged when they see each other 30 minutes later. Further, words and actions for greetings differ, depending on whether the child is

greeting a teacher or a peer. Greetings are complex, as are most social skills."

Social Understanding and Imagination:

Do you find yourself wondering how can your child be so selfish while playing? He/she is the first to tell others off for being so. The lack of social imagination—commonly observed in children with autism—should not be confused as lack of imagination. Children with autism can be imaginative and creative in an area of interest, and can excel thanks to their gift and talent. But social imagination is different. Social imagination helps us understand and predict other people's behavior. Have you ever gone to an unknown place that was difficult to imagine, or had situations outside your immediate daily routine? For a child with autism this is a fact of his/her life. He/she has a lot of trouble working out what other people believe or think. They cannot make sense of abstract ideas, and guessing what other people think it is too difficult for them. So your child may run on to a busy road not because he lacks discipline. He doesn't understand the concept of danger in that situation, and he may think that all this noise is dangerous and must be escaped. You may hear your child asking you in distress what will happen in the future. Acting out the same scenes again and again prepares such children for upcoming change, and helps in planning for future unfamiliar situations.

So children with autism may find it difficult to determine and interpret other people's thoughts, feelings and actions, and to foresee what will or might occur next. They often cannot identify hazards or engage in imaginative play and activities. Although they enjoy some imaginative play, they have a strong preference to act out familiar scenes that they understand. This helps them prepare for change and plan for the future. It also helps to cope in new or unfamiliar situations which may cause stress. These are the same reasons why they find it difficult to develop interpersonal play. Consequently, they might have a limited range of imaginative activities, possibly ones that are copied rigidly and repetitively.

Therefore, your child may play by using a hand flapping or ritualized action. He/she doesn't always understand a different point of view because he/she has difficulties imaging or planning the future. This causes them to repetitively copy roles without understanding what they are doing. Repetitive behaviors can sometimes take the form of obsessions and their content might be unusual for the child's age or their depth of knowledge. The child could be interested in strange objects as vacuum cleaners, symbols, or numbers. His/her thoughts are often inflexible and unconnected. For example, when this child sees a toy car, what he/she really sees is an object that rattles when its wheels are spun. Your child's need for sameness may extend to his/her food. That's the reason they dislike or love certain colors or textures of foods. These behavioral patterns typically characterize the clinical entity of autism.

However, it must be emphasized that the presentation of autistic behavior varies among individuals. Even in the same individual, the clinical picture differs, depending on age and mental capability. Remember that each child is unique, and the best way to approach your children is to interact with them and understand their particular way of learning. Every education program being applied should assess and consider the triad of impairments that represent the particular clinical entity of autism.

Despite the difficulties, let's keep in mind words of a person with autism:

> "Sad to say, there is a disability with Asperger Syndrome but it's not all mine. You cannot have a communication disorder without at least two people. It is a question I wish more people would ask me. Perhaps then there would be less ignorance and a little understanding and tolerance. And I wouldn't have to live my life pretending to be normal."

Chapter summary

Recognizing your child's difficulties associated with social behavior provide an early diagnosis and intervention. Children with autism interpret social life like a complicated game where they are the only who haven't been told the rules. They develop deviant language and communication abilities. But this doesn't mean that they don't have the desire to be with others. These children can be imaginative and creative in an area of interest, but often lack social imagination. Children with autism find it hard to understand and predict other people's behavior. Thus every education program being applied should assess and consider the triad of impairments for the particular child.

Chapter 4
The causes of autism

In 1949, Leo Kanner studied atypical children and stated that children with autism were born into high status families and described their mothers as 'refrigerator mothers'. Autism was attributed to the cold mothering style because of the limited sample of Kanner's study. (1, 2, 15) A year later, Bruno Bettleheim also claimed that autism was an emotional disorder due to the psychological harm of mother's parental style.

In 1964 Bernard Rimland—whose father had autism—disagreed with the claim that bad parenting caused autism, and instead he focused on biological conditions. Rimland is credited with abolishing the notion that distant mothers were responsible for autism, and as a consequence had a strong impact on the available treatment programs.

Schopler and Reichler (1971) studied the effects of parents on children in treatment and found that parental acceptance of having a child with autism affected the child's behavior. In 1977, the first published study with identical twins was reported by Susan Folstein and Michael Rutter. Using 21 same sexed twin pairs, where at least one twin had autism, they suggested out that brain injury in infancy may lead to autism, with or without a genetic predisposition. In 1980, autism was added to diagnostic and Statistical Manual of Mental Disorders – III as "Infantile Autism". This provided clear criteria for diagnosis. It also gave the opportunity for diagnosis of autism and importantly, the differentiation of autism from schizophrenia.

Most of these notions are not just out-dated today, but also emphatically disproved. Their only real value is in reassuring parents today that they did NOT cause their child to have autism. In their time, most of these theories—particularly the ones that held mothers responsible—have caused a great deal of trauma to parents, and affected the parent-child relationship. As more research managed to show the flaws in these theories, it became more evident that the causes of autism are more complex than previously believed.

The exact cause of autism is still unknown, but all professionals in the field agree that the qualitative deviation of autistic symptoms are of organic origin, and seem to be associated with brain malfunction. Biochemical and structural malfunctions seems implicated, as it then affects the brain mechanisms of sensory processing. This impact is found to be different in different individuals.

Recent research suggests that the autistic spectrum disorders are neurodevelopmental disorders stemming from an irregularity in the brain's initial development. Studies of people with autism have found irregularities in several brain regions. Researchers have identified a number of genes associated with the disorder (although how these genes interact to cause autism is still being explored). They have identified a number of rare genetic changes or *mutations* associated with autism. Most cases involve a complex and variable combination of genetic risk and environmental factors that influence brain development; making the task of identifying cause even more challenging.

All this research suggests that autism is caused by complex interactions among a number of factors, and that the blame cannot yet be laid squarely at the door of any one reason. Parents need to be informed about the causes of autism, and the complex—yet unpredictable—interactions that seem to occur. Appropriate information not only exonerates them from guilt or self-blame, but also gives them the opportunity to choose educational programs that fit their child's needs.

Chapter summary

In spite of tremendous research, the exact cause of autism is still unknown. What the scientists do know, is that qualitative deviation and autistic symptoms are of organic etiology, and due to brain malfunction. Biochemical and structural malfunctions affect different individuals in different ways. Appropriate information about causes of autism not only allows parents to stop blaming themselves, but also gives them the opportunity to choose the educational programs that are the best fit for their child.

Chapter 5
From diagnosis to treatment: An ongoing process

Beginning with a diagnosis

A diagnosis is a label that helps professionals to describe a number of symptomatic behaviors. Did you ever feel that the label has no meaning for you as a parent? Diagnosis is the first step in a long journey, and it proves to be an important turning point. Remember, this is not just a label that your child gets; how you view it determines the direction of the journey. It depends on you and the professionals you meet to not view it as a "punishment" or "a tragedy" for your family. (6, 11)

An early diagnosis may help you make sense of things or behaviors you already knew about. As you are the person who spends most time with your child, you will be able to appreciate the value of knowing what each symptom represents. An early diagnosis may bring you sadness, but it is also a cause for relief, since it can explain your child's behavior.

Even before the diagnosis, you will have already noticed his/her difficulties in interacting with people and things, with paying attention, and looking aloof. You may have already noticed the repetitive interests that absorb him/her, and have already dealt with his/her resistance to doing things differently. You have already dealt with challenging behaviors such as putting inedible items in the mouth, and pinching or other self-injurious behavior. Often, it's these issues that prompt parents to seek help.

Once the diagnosis explains the reasons for these behaviors, it can be the first step in helping you and your child improve your relationship. At this point, it's important to feel that you are not alone. Talk to other parents or professionals who embrace and empathize with your mixed feelings and help guide you. They can give you hope and a reason to remain strong. It's important to remember that your child remains the same lovable person he/she was before the diagnosis.

Some parents may choose not to get a formal diagnosis as they prefer not to think it as a disability. It's OK to not apply a label, but this should not mean that the child does not receive the educational programs that he/she needs. Not having a formal diagnosis should not mean that the unique needs of the child are ignored. It is helpful not to see your child as disabled, but appropriate information and intervention may prove to be crucial for his/her development.

Diagnosis of autism isn't a simple task. Diagnosis is a part of the overall assessment. Parents become aware of the strengths and weaknesses of their children from a full assessment. If diagnosis is the first step, the assessment is an ongoing process that helps your child to grow up. There are no individual tests to confirm a diagnosis of Autism Spectrum Disorder. Consider autism and the range of clinical characteristics your child shows. The diagnosis comes from an overview of a number of evaluations conducted by a multidisciplinary team. This team may consist of:

- A developmental pediatrician who already knows the child's development

- A psychiatrist

- A psychologist

- A speech/language therapist

- A neurologist

- An audiologist

- An occupational therapist

Through these evaluations, other neurological syndromes or hearing problems can be eliminated from the spectrum of possibilities. Furthermore, you can get a full assessment of your child's weaknesses and strengths based on language, behavior, cognitive ability, social interaction. Thanks to these evaluations, the special therapist who leads the team can create a complete educational program that depends on your child's unique needs.

A typical evaluation would begin by initially raising concerns about your child to a language therapist, family doctor, or school practitioner. These health professionals can then refer the child for assessment by specialists as mentioned above. Once a comprehensive assessment has been conducted, then a program—based on the information gathered by all health professionals involved—can be developed for your child, and treatment can begin.

For more information about the diagnostic criteria, you can visit sites like www.autismspeaks.org/what-autism/diagnosis or https://www.autismspeaks.org/what-autism/diagnosis/dsm-5-diagnostic-criteria. There is also some information on these criteria given in the appendix.

Chapter summary

An early diagnosis may give a name or an explanation for issues or behaviors that parents already knew. A diagnosis is the first step to helping your child and improving your relationship with him/her. Different parents react differently to a diagnosis of autism, and there is no 'correct' response. Diagnosis is just a part of the assessment. The assessment is an ongoing process that helps your child as he/she grows up. Multidisciplinary teams can conduct a number of evaluations in order to reach to a valid diagnosis.

Chapter 6
Intervention and treatment methods ([4], [16], [17])

Your child is unique, so the treatment program you follow needs to be be just as unique and addressed to the needs and strengths of your child. That's why a full assessment is necessary before an intervention program is designed. Treatment for autism involves a group of professionals and the entire family. As Temple Grandin states: ([13])

> "A treatment method or an educational method that will work for one child may not work for another child. The one common denominator for all of the young children is that early intervention does work and it seems to improve prognosis."

Parents sometimes feel trapped as there are plenty of treatment programs available. There is no point in choosing a program for your child if it doesn't address to his/her daily needs or it doesn't enhance the child's strengths. That's why it's important to know your child and use all the available information you have for your child before making the choice. Treatment programs for autism spectrum disorder can be divided into different categories related to the goals and the behavioral patterns/symptoms a child develops. The educational plan of your child could have some of the following treatment categories.

Behavior and Development Programs

The choice of Behavior and Development programs depends on the child's age, and his/her needs. Social skills, attention, challenging behaviors, play, emotions and parent interaction can be addressed through these programs.

Education and Learning Programs

These programs are usually applied through schools or special education centers. Their main goal is to improve learning and enhance reasoning skills that would be useful throughout life. Although schools and centers may use different names for the programs applied, their philosophy is usually based either on the 'Treatment and Education of Autistic and Communication

Related Handicapped Children' approach (TEACCH) or on the 'Applied Behavior Analysis' programs that emphasize positive reinforcement for learning goals. TEACCH programs are based on the use of visual cues that help the learning process in a classroom arrangement.

Medication

There is no consensus on the use of medicine for autism spectrum disorders. It's a fact that medication can not treat autism. There are some drugs such as Risperidone or Aripiprazole that are used in the case of severe autistic symptoms for reducing aggression, hyperactivity and self-injury, but these are basically used to manage situations, and are not a cure. As it is, before taking any medication, it's important to consult a child psychiatrist specialized in dealing with autism who already knows the child well. In addition to medication, symptoms of depression, anxiety, attention deficits or hyperactivity should also be considered through management of the environmental conditions associated with the symptoms.

Other treatment and therapies

Speech and language therapy, music therapy, occupational therapy, acupuncture, vitamins and mineral supplements, massage therapy are some alternative treatments that could help your child. However, this doesn't mean that all children need all these therapies, or will benefit from them. Discussing alternative treatments with other parents could prove to be helpful in getting new ideas and perspectives. Before applying any alternative therapy, it is always better to discuss it with your therapist who has a general oversight of your child. Any program that is applied to your child will be effective only if it fits into his/her needs.

Parent education programs

It is common all the therapies should be addressed to the children's needs. Nevertheless, for their success, parents should participate in the educational programs too. Every program, either educational or behavioral, should be applied to the home. The special trainer who works with the child will not be at the home, which is why parents need to know all about autism and follow the same treatment approach in their interaction with the child. They should be informed of how all these programs can be implemented and incorporated into the child's daily routine. For example, if a child learns an alternative communication system as PECS or MAKATON, there is no benefit if parents aren't trained for this.

Post diagnosis decisions

Soon after the formal diagnosis, a decision should be made about the programs that you and your child will attend. As a parent, you may feel confused or overwhelmed by your feelings and you need to be guided by your therapists. However, you will need to make the final decisions, as you can best decide what programs can be effectively implemented. These are some useful questions to ask your therapists that will help you to make the optimal choice for you and your child.

- Which program is the best for my child, taking into account his/her needs?

- Which intervention program would help my child?

- What is available for me and my child in the region I live?

- What about school? Are there school programs in my community which address the needs of children with autism?

- What's the cost?

- Are there any educational programs applied from public services?

- Who is a good speech therapist for my child's needs?

- Does my health insurance cover any of these costs?

- What are the changes in our daily life that we should be making?

- What else can we do to help our child?

Chapter summary

The treatment program you follow should be addressed to the needs and strengths of your child. There is no benefit to your child following a treatment program that doesn't address to his/her daily needs. For a treatment program to work, you as parents need to get involved and apply the program in your own household.

Chapter 7
Living with a child with autism (2, 7, 15, 21)

"I always knew that my child was different", says a mother of an 8 year old autistic child.

> "Gina as infant never made eye contact. She didn't look for me or my husband. She was a quiet baby and she paid no attention to us. I never heard her call me mama and she didn't have interest in playing the peek-a-boo game. Although we knew that something was wrong, it was a shock to hear on her third birthday that she had autism. I didn't even know what autism was. Neither did my husband. We felt sad, angry, terrified and uncertain about her future and our life with her. Inevitably, although the period of diagnosis was a harsh time for us, it proved to be a turning point in our relationship with her. Of course it wasn't easy to admit that my daughter is autistic. Stepping away from my emotions, I began to think of her and how lonely she could feel in a place where no one understands her. I didn't want to let her down. After few months of attending an early intervention program, we felt more in control. We can understand our daughter now and she learns more and more about the world. She remains our loving and beautiful daughter with an autistic side, and we embrace it even though sometimes it's hard.

Parents' concerns for children who have autism are quite extensive. They are worried for the child's future as well as their present. Parents often worry about quality of life, financial well-being, employment and housing needs, education, independence, and longevity of life.

These are the same concerns that most parents have for their children—regardless of whether the child has any challenge. But there are many qualitative differences in the concerns of other parents and parents of children with autism. Apart from financial challenges raised by treatment programs, they have to respond to a daily routine which can be both time consuming and tiring. Preparing for school, getting breakfast, brushing their teeth, or taking a nap are greater concerns than for other parents. Sometimes they have to fight or move to another city even for their educational rights. Living with a child with autism is a daily challenge that a parent learns to deal with. Even when they recognize and accept that autism is just one part of their child, they have to cope with a lot of issues like medical issues, seizures, regression, behavioral problems, medication, sleep disturbances, sibling and family issues, sensory issues. This leaves parents of children with autism less time to prepare for their child's future, and thus each small setback can leave them more overwhelmed about what adulthood has in store for their child.

Seizures

There are studies which suggest that seizures affect an increasingly high number of children with autism. Seizures are caused by abnormal electrical activity in the brain. They provoke a temporary loss of consciousness, body convulsions, unusual movements and/or staring spells. High fever or lack of sleep can produce seizures. People with autism develop seizures more often than the general population—both as children, and as adults. Thus, parents should be informed about this possibility. If seizure activity is recurrent, it may be necessary to talk about epilepsy. Anticonvulsants are proven to be effective in reducing or preventing seizures. Parents should be aware of how seizure medicine affects their children's behavior and should discuss options with their doctor.

The signs warning of a seizure include unexplained staring spells, stiffening of muscles, involuntary jerking of limbs, facial twitching, unexplained confusion severe headaches sleepiness or sleep disturbances, marked and unexplained irritability or aggressiveness, and regression in normal development

Regression (9)

Regression simply means going back to a lower ability level after demonstrating a higher one. Early diagnosis of autism doesn't involve the presence of abnormal behaviors, but the absence of normal developmental steps. There are a number of children with autism who make significant progress in social communication and acquisition of language during the first year of life and then suddenly experience a loss of these abilities. These children sometimes manage eye contact or babbling as infants, and then, in a dramatic way, they lose these abilities. Regression is an important warning sign, and if an early diagnosis is made, there can be a better prognosis for a child's development.

Behavioral Problems (5, 7)

Challenging behaviors are the most stressful characteristic of autism that parents have to deal with. As a parent, you may feel stressed and blame yourself every time your child runs away screams while covering his/her ears, refuses to wear clothes, throws or spits his/her food, bites others, or hits himself/herself. Challenging behaviors are all these behavioral patterns which are harmful, destructive, prevent learning and cause isolation.

These behaviors are sometimes the result of internal factors, and sometimes external factors. It helps to keep in mind that autism itself cannot cause challenging behaviors. These behaviors are caused by feelings of frustration and the pain that difficulties evoke when the child feels unable to do something that they want to. Challenging behaviors are a sign that the child is unhealthy or unhappy, and they represent the only possible reaction your child feels capable of at the time.

Understanding what triggers your child's behaviors is the key to dealing with them. This will involve figuring out your child's needs, and searching for the hidden meaning of the behaviors. One must examine the external environment, looking for social triggers, stimulation issues, communication problems, and lack of interest issues. One must search for sources of pain, seizures, food allergies and sensitivities, basic needs for food or water, negative feelings, or coordination problems as well. Ideal responses to the situation will help in stabilizing senses and regulating emotions.

Sleep Disturbances

Children with autism may face sleep problems that affect attention, mood and learning process. As with any other concerns, the cause should be found out. Some children develop sleep problems because of medical issues that need to be addressed. Obstructive sleep apnea or gastro esophageal reflux, allergies or seizures can also cause sleep problems. If there are no medical problems, keeping a daily diary can help you implement a daily routine so the child can sleep on a regular basis. For some children, limiting the amount of sleep during the day could be helpful.

Sensory issues

Senses help us to be informed about the external world. The central nervous system processes all the sensory information we receive from the external world. Smells, sounds, touches, tastes, sights, balance—all give us information, and thanks to the brain, we can organize and prioritize this information. Our behavior is the response to all these stimuli.

Many (not all) children with autism have difficulties processing all this everyday sensory information. Trying to respond to it, they may feel anxious and even feel physical pain. Challenging behaviors can be a result of dissatisfaction caused by sensory integration difficulties. You may wonder why your child has particular eating habits or attention issues. He/she may insist on not wearing specific clothes, or has difficulties sleeping. You may feel devastated when you see him chew everything or smear things. But these are the harbingers of sensory dysfunction. Typical examples include being overly sensitive to stimuli, not reacting to stimuli, (e.g. a sudden noise doesn't scare him), being easily distracted, having many social and emotional problems, being clumsy, overactive or hyperactive, hating changes, and/or being unable to calm him/herself.

Being aware of the annoying sensory stimuli could prove to be helpful in order to avoid them or finding out ways for bringing calmness. Even small environmental changes can release your child from the pressure and the pain he/she feels. The general principles of dealing with sensory dysfunction are: being aware of the difficulties, being prepared to deal with them and being creative with replacing the distress of negative experiences with positive sensory experiences

If your child is under-sensitive, try to give him/her stimuli that make him/her feel alert. On the other hand, if your child is hypersensitive to stimuli, try to reduce the stimuli in his/her surroundings by using auxiliary assets. For example, if a child is sensitive to visual stimuli, giving them sunglasses to wear and explaining their use could help. Occupational therapy and music therapy can also prove to be helpful for over or under sensitive children.

Chapter summary

Living with a child with autism is a daily challenge. Even when parents recognize and accept that autism is a part of their child, they have to manage a lot of issues like seizures, regression, behavioral problems, medication, sleep disturbances, sibling and family issues, and sensory issues. It helps to be creative and gather information for dealing with all these issues, since help is available. The trick is to find what works for each particular child.

Chapter 8
The grief cycle (<u>14</u>, <u>17</u>)

After the diagnosis, you as a parent have to deal with your own feelings. Having a child with autism is a challenge, and in order to raise a happy child, you should be aware of your own feelings. Self awareness is the key to not feeling overwhelmed, to make decisions for you and your child, and to keep your family in balance.

Family systems theories underline the importance of viewing the family as a unit. Each individual plays an important role in the family as a whole. At the same time, even though the actions of one family member do influence the actions of the others, it is important for each member to also be able to differentiate themselves from the others.

Families whose members stand as unique entities are more able to manage stress and adapt to changes, since their emotional states are less enmeshed. There is a study that indicates that parents of children with autism show fewer symptoms of depression and somatic problems when they are able to seek social support and speak about their mixed feelings. They also have lower rates of anxiety and stress. This study underlines the need for awareness of your negative feelings and sharing them with your partner.

Furthermore, being aware of the grief cycle can help you to accept your child's uniqueness. Even though you and your family have to struggle with many difficulties and ambiguous feelings, it is nevertheless possible for you to live in a healthy atmosphere. Most researchers claim that parents may deal with the emotions of loss after a diagnosis. The emotional state is considered comparable to the grief process that one might undergo with the death of a close family member. But there is a basic difference. In the case of a death, people must deal with the cold absence of their loved one without hope for a new set of experiences. But when a child has autism, the parents must deal with losing the belief that their child is 'normal', and they need to understand what this means for their family. You may have heard parents say how hard it was when they first heard that their child had autism. At first, they couldn't believe it. A tremendous sense of loss may have accompanied these feelings, but they still need to continue to care for the child and understand how to best help him/her.

The way people grieve after a death differs. Just as there is no right or wrong way to grieve after a death, there is no right or wrong way to react when you hear that your child has autism. Some people hold in their emotions and thoughts, while others feel overwhelmed and look for support from friends, family or specialists.

Typical responses include disbelief, shock, denial, relief, fear, anger, sadness, and despair. Many parents may feel lost in terms of this mysterious and unknown word "autism". Eventually, they will have a lot of questions; but it can be unbelievably hard for them to find the right words to ask these questions. Being overwhelmed by emotions and feeling "stoned" is a natural reaction that indicates the beginning of the grief process.

Elizabeth Kubler Ross and Kessler suggest that after a death, there are five stages that someone may go through. These stages are part of an ongoing process and include Denial, Anger, Bargaining, Sadness/Depression, and Acceptance. There is no a specific order and it is not certain that everyone who grieves will pass through all these stages. Remember that there is no right or wrong way to grieve.

The same emotions affect parents when they first hear that their children have autism. One does not need to be afraid of these feelings. They help a person process and accept reality, and consequently, build a healthy relationship with the child. It is a painful process, but it will help you bury the dreams or expectations of the ideal child. Although it feels like the end, expressing all these feelings is helpful in accepting facts and forming fresh dreams for one's child.

Denial

Denial presents itself through a variety of thoughts, and a person can have one or more of these.

You may think that this is not your child.

You may think that your child isn't developmentally harmed.

You may think that the doctor is mistaken.

You may think that your child will comply and 'change'.

You may think that there will be a miracle.

You may think that nobody knows your child better than you, not even specialists.

You may think that your child will change when he/she grows up.

Parents often suspect that something is different with their child as they notice that non-typical development even before diagnosis. It is a common reaction to ignore all the signs that suggest autism. Don't blame yourself for the time you pass being in denial. Denial is a normal and healthy reaction when you have to cope with (usually negative) life changing events. A diagnosis of autism is a life changing event for both, child and parent. Everyone needs time to process the news, and so it is absolutely normal to deny the reality at a subconscious level. Parents need this time in order to prepare themselves for raising a child with autism. Denial at the first stages of a diagnosis is a coping mechanism that gives parents time to cope. That's why parents don't need to feel guilty about the time spent in denial, or blame themselves for neglecting their child. Just as there are no perfect children, there are no perfect parents. Raising a child with autism needs time and strength, and denial allows the time needed to prepare and get stronger for the many struggles ahead.

Gathering information and learning about autism may prove to be a productive way to deal with your emotions and thoughts during the phase of denial. But denial may prove to be pathological if parents continue ignoring the diagnosis and believing that their child is normal. Such parents continue to distance themselves from friends, relatives or professionals who try to talk about it. As a result the child doesn't attend therapeutic or educational programs, and this has a negative effect on his/her growth and his/her relationships with others.

Anger

Do you feel so angry that you swear aloud or break things?

Do you feel so angry that you are convinced that you hate everyone?

Do you and your spouse have fights for no reason?

Do you feel angry with life for being so hard on you and your child?

Anger is a normal emotion that rises after the diagnosis. After a diagnosis, anger helps parents to get out of denial and deal with the situation. It activates them and encourages them to find information that will help them take control the situation. Although one tends to distance others or feel isolated when angry, it is necessary to keep in mind that others can actually help you make sense of the reality. When you first hear that your child has autism, you may direct your anger to your friends, family, professionals, other parents or even towards yourself and your child. Processing your anger provides you the opportunity to go forward.

Parents can feel angry years after the diagnosis. but the frequency with which they feel angry, the circumstances under which they feel angry, and the way they deal with it changes over time. It doesn't help to suppress anger. Suppressing feelings can result in emotional outbursts or in isolation. It's OK to be angry. Discuss your anger with someone you trust without guilt. This will help you to leave behind all the negative thoughts and find more creative ideas to take action. Refocusing your anger into something positive keeps you going till you find the optimal strategies for your family instead of hurting them.

Bargaining

There is some point that parents may begin bargaining. Typical statements include:

If I am a good parent, my child will be neurotypical.

If I believe in God, my child will magically begin to talk

If I follow the instructions that psychologist gave me, my child will make eye contact.

If I...If I...

Coping with feelings of anger or despair, parents bargain with themselves, higher powers or professionals. They are willing to give up something precious or do something in order to change their child's condition. Bargaining helps parents to remain optimistic, and to not to lose hope as they see their child deal with his/her daily difficulties. All the information about autism can make them feel powerless, making them want to restore hope and strength by appealing to "higher powers". They may idealize the clinicians they visit and ascribe magical and unrealistic powers to them. Deep inside, they might believe that their child will be cured and the autism will magically disappear. Accepting the reality that autism is not curable, and that it is a developmental disability that the child will have to cope with all their lives, isn't an easy step. What waiting for miracles does do, is buy parents time till they find other, more realistic sources of remaining optimistic and hopeful.

It helps to start learning about autism. Gathering information and learning helps parents feel powerful and less confused. They feel more in control and stop bargaining with higher intelligences, once they realize that there is a lot that they can do for their child to help them become the best adjusted versions of themselves.

Depression

Dealing with a child's autism is exhausting. There are times you may feel that there is no point fighting against it all. There are times you may feel disappointed and think that everything you do is useless. There are times you may feel like being left alone, and there are times when the loneliness is crushing. There are times you may feel that your child lives in a trashy and messy world and you have to accept this hard situation.

After the diagnosis, and as time passes by, parents often express feelings of depression and disappointment. Living with a child with autism and his/her difficulties, not knowing how to cope, and seeing other children progressing faster, can make a parent feel helpless and lonely. For parents, the cycle of grief can seem endless. Parents notice that their children don't grow like other kids or that they lose developmental milestones. Watching their child unable to speak or play in a typical manner may bring sadness and pain. It seems sometimes that parents have to grieve for every developmental step that their child doesn't achieve. Admitting their child's lifelong disability raises some strong and mixed feelings including fear of the unknown, and sadness.

Expressing all these feelings can help parents to overcome their obstacles and build a healthy relationship with their child. They may still grieve or feel depressed at times in their life. Chronic depression isn't the same thing as the depressive feelings someone may feel during the grief process. Chronic depression is a serious mental illness that needs intervention. The depression that parents feel after a diagnosis of autism is normal. Accepting all these feelings and dealing with them is the first step to moving on.

It's OK to let yourself cry. Crying may prove to be liberating and helps release pent up emotions. Pampering yourself by doing something fun or comforting apart from dealing with autism may also help you release the depressive feelings.

Acceptance

As time passes, people learn to adapt to new perspectives and actions. Do you sometimes catch yourself saying "this is my child" with the same pride as other parents? Do you feel that there is a place in this world for him/her despite the difficulties posited by autism? Do you see her/his abilities and strengths more clearly? Do you feel that you will do anything to give him/her the life she/he deserves?

When a parent stops questioning "why did this happen to me", it means that he/she has begun to accept the child's diagnosis and has started coping with all the changes to come. Processing the negative feelings and finding a way to express their thoughts helps parents move forward and realize that there is still a way to enjoy life and parenthood.

Now parents can focus on understanding their child, rather than on what he/she can't become. Thus, they start to leave behind some of the anger, blame, guilt and fear. They still wonder how they can make it all work for the best, but they have begun to believe in their strengths.

Acceptance is not as easy as it sounds, and parents first need support for grieving the child they will never have. There is a point at which parents accept that autism is just a part of their child's life and they can continue living while dealing with their emotions. Parents now realize that their challenges don't have typical solutions, but they feel satisfied because they are able to make it through. They accept that it's OK to have all these emotions and when they see the child, they see a person and not a disability.

Jim Sinclair, an adult with autism, in his article "Don't Mourn For Us" speaks of the cycle of grief parents experience after a diagnosis. He encourages parents to grieve for their lost dreams, but not to mourn for their children as mourning is not needed. In 1993, at the presentation Jim Sinclair gave at the International Conference on Autism in Toronto, he went on record to say that the process starts with acknowledging who the child is not. It is OK to grieve for lost dreams by exploring the expectations that parents usually have for a child. He asks parents to say the following: (22)

> "This is not my child that I expected and planned for. This is not the child I waited for through all those months of pregnancy and all those hours of labor. This is not the child I made all those plans to share all these experiences with. That child never came. This is not that child."

But after grieving this dream—which he asks parents to keep away from their children—it is time to let go and start anew. He encourages parents to explore how their child is different from them and then accept these differences as part of their parenting process. He says:

> ...say to yourself: "This is not my child that I expected and planned for. This is an alien child who landed in my life by accident. I don't know who this child is or what it will become. But I know it's a child, stranded in an alien world, without parents of its own kind to care for it. It needs someone to care for it, to teach it, to interpret and to advocate for it. And because this alien child happened to drop into my life, that job is mine if I want it."

Chapter summary

After a diagnosis, parents may deal with the emotions of loss. The cycle of grief that most parents experience includes the emotional states of denial, anger, bargaining, depression and acceptance. All these feelings are normal. Expressing all these feelings help parents to see, as time passes, that an autism diagnosis is not the end. Although acceptance is not as easy as it sounds, and parents need support for grieving the child they will never have, there is nevertheless hope for a happier and productive life ahead for both parent and child.

Chapter 9
Strategies for parenting child with autism (<u>3</u>, <u>10</u>, <u>14</u>, <u>19</u>, <u>20</u>)

Bringing a child with autism into the world is a life changing event for most parents. Parents who manage to deal with their feelings and create a strong bond with their child can fare well and live in a healthy family system. There are studies suggesting that parents of children with autism show more chance of developing higher stress levels. This happens due to the child's autistic behavioral characteristics, the difficulty in getting a diagnosis, and the barriers to accessing social support.

If you are raising a child with autism, you know that a diagnosis of autism may disrupt your emotional, physical, social and family life, but despite the initial shock, you may find that you can receive unexpected joys while dealing with the challenges of raising a child with autism. These unique children can give you unpretentious love as long as they feel safe and understood, and can turn parenting into an unexpected treasure hunt. Here are some tested pointers to a happier interaction with your child:

Keep faith in your child's and your family's abilities: Having a positive perspective helps you to discover your child's abilities and offset his/her disabilities. Paying attention to the positive aspects of the child's development and not focusing on the problems empowers the family to act in an effective way.

Being aware of stressful situations and coping strategies: This helps in not losing faith and enables you to continue to cooperate with professionals. There will be times you may feel disappointed or tired of all these intervention programs and specialists, and dream of a life without them. Talking about and sharing your feelings with them may give relief. Taking into account your feelings, professionals may find ways to comfort you. Don't forget that you being happy and calm, helps your child to be the same.

Encourage the development of specific talents of your child: Developing talents based on their interests helps enhance his/her self-esteem and peer acceptance. Watching him/her being happy and focused on his/her special interests will be a source of calmness for you as well.

Be flexible with problem solving techniques and ideas. Something that works for one child, may not work for another. Even something that was effective for your child's learning before, may not continue to stay effective. Creativity and flexibility make parenting a more challenging experience; but with practice it can open doors to valuable outcomes for your family.

Your child can learn: With the right intervention plan and lots of love and support, most children with autism can learn quite well.

Learn about autism: Knowledge helps to deal with all strong feelings and banish fears. As a parent, knowledge can provide you with some sense of control

Accept your child's "weirdness" rather than trying to extinguish it: All these quirks are part of your child. Comparing your child to others makes him/her feel lonely and not accepted.

Don't give in to pessimism and negative feelings: Your child isn't fated to a handicapped life. He/she just needs time to grow and expand his/her unique wings.

Choosing schooling programs: A dilemma than many parents confront is school inclusion, and a choice between mainstream and special education programs. Integration and school inclusion is unquestionably a right for your child. Most countries encourage the idea of mainstreaming children with autism in regular schools. Nevertheless, school inclusion should not be unconditional. The conditions of mainstreaming a child with autism to general classes should be cautiously looked into. Unconditional integration may prove to be a disaster for your child's well being. Some parents feel that if their child attends regular classes, he/she will be (mis)treated as a "normal" child. Full inclusion should be used where possible, but parents should keep in mind that a child's happiness should not be sacrificed for the idea of being normal and equal. Parents, teachers and professionals (psychologists, social workers, occupational therapists, speech therapists and doctors) should make a full individual assessment of the child's abilities and disabilities after taking into account the school environment and resources. Through this assessment, parents can seek potential options that would positively influence their children. Keep in mind that your child's happiness is the best criterion to understand in which school environment he/she belongs.

Get a strong social support: Having a child with autism doesn't mean you need to isolate yourself from others. You are not just a parent, but also a friend, brother, sister, son, daughter, partner, and husband or wife. Your relationships with other people are essential to help you cope with the challenges awaiting you.

Be cautious: It is tempting to consider a therapy that claims to be a miracle cure for autism. But treading with caution is recommended with all these therapies for autism.

Plan time for breaks: When you have free time, try to spend it as you like. This won't solve your problems or eliminate negative emotions, but it gives you the chance to rest and think clearly. Schedule your restricted free time with activities you and your partner enjoy.

Don't be afraid to get inside your child's world. Getting inside will help you to obtain a better insight of his/her needs, and to appreciate their joys and concerns. It also helps accept the fact that your child only really needs to be unconditionally loved and accepted.